POLAROIDS OF TURBULENCE

POLAROIDS OF TURBULENCE

HENRY SUSSMAN

BLAZEVOX[BOOKS]
Buffalo, New York

Interior design and typesetting by Geoffrey Gatza
Cover artwork and interspersed: Australian paintings from the permanent collections of the Art
Gallery of New South Wales, Sydney, Australia. Cover design by Geoffrey Gatza. All images ©
Copyright Agency. Licensed by Artists Rights Society (ARS), New York, 2024:
Frontispiece: "Warlugulong," by Clifford Possum Tpaltjarri and Tim Leura Tpaltjarri (1976).
p. 82: "Untitled (Jupiter Well to Tjukula)," by Uta Uta Tjukula (1979).
p. 91: "Water and Wallaby Dreaming," by Dick Pantimatus Tjupurrula (1981).

First Edition
ISBN: 978-1-60964-458-1
Library of Congress Control Number: 2023950170

BlazeVOX [books]
131 Euclid Ave
Kenmore, NY 14217
Editor@blazevox.org

publisher of weird little books

BlazeVOX [books]

blazevox.org

BlazeVOX

Acknowledgements:

"Morning Fog" appeared in *Epiphany* (2016).

"Atlas of Vanished Places," "Co-lateral Dommages," and "Three Deer in a Development near Harrisburg, PA" appeared in my *The Great Dismissal: Memoir of the Cultural Demolition Derby, 2015-22* (Bloomsbury Academic, 2023).

While the texts in this volume emerged to me over the better part of a lifetime, it was not until 2005 that I connected to the living community of poetry. My work has been multifariously nurtured and enhanced through my participation in "First Tuesdays" at Express 77 in Jackson Heights, as curated by Richard Jeffrey Newman and enriched, month after month, by its gifted core of regulars. As it was from 2005 to 2015 by being part of the Yale Working Group in Poetry and Poetics, under the revelatory illumination issuing from Jean-Jacques Poucel, Richard Deming, Nancy Kuhl, David Mahan, and invited guests. Rather than being an arid detour away from my project, the COVID-19 shutdown of 2020-22 turned out surprisingly affirmative and productive. This was in large measure because I was able to connect up with and participate in two online reading series: the Enclave readings, curated by Rae Armantrout and Jeanne Heuving; and IAWA, The Italian-American Writers Association in its online phase, coordinated by Maria Lisella, Julia Lisella, and Jenn Martelli.

Since 2018, a bevy of gifted readers has lent its wisdom, craft, and skill to individual pieces collected here. Two of my most incisive critics were once students in graduate seminars I offered at SUNY-Buffalo: Andrea Strudensky and Linda Reinfeld. Elizabeth Gray Jr. has proven unstinting in critiquing my style and in orienting me to the wider universe of poetry, as has Richard Jeffrey Newman. David Siller, Jay Brodbar, Steve Getlein, Mark Kerson, Victor Vatyas, and Ann Vise have all channeled indispensable gut reactions and wisdom through the arduous group exercise of line-by-line workshopping. And at the very outset of this experiment, in the late 1960's, I gained enduring poetic perspective from two instructors, Allen Grossman and Howard Nemerov, and a classmate, Michael Rosenthal--ever since an unfailing lightening-rod of the new and noteworthy on the contemporary scene. Geoffrey Gatza, Kristina Darling, Roger Craik, and all associated with BlazeVOX [books] made the experience of publishing *Polaroids of Turbulence* uplifting and transformative throughout.

Contents

POLAROIDS OF TURBULENCE

Directions

Proceed
directly,
always,
to the node
of pain.
Where
you're
needed.

Thought alone
never
saves you—
only cata
clysmic
aftershock,
seismic after
thought,
pain-level,
"infinity."

Withstand this stream,
discomfiting
disclosure—
to live.

Evade, avoid—
and you dis
solve--anti
matter, anti
self--what you
prided
yourself
tran
scending.

Morning Fog

at the outerbanks of
introspection, diminish
ing shoal, as the orb
gathers fluid, virtual
maze of sources,
very limit of surface
tension. Com
posit organism
stretches its semi
permeable
membrane.

Death-machines
have cleared the rearview
mirror.

The shore
huddled. The tide
gathers.

Homeland

                                                            Old man,
possibly worse for a couple
drinks, stumbling.

On the lilt--
some sentimental tune persisting
from the homeland—
always sought, never
quite inhabited.

His viscous voice,
spicy from the years,
incessant humming,
maybe it's really the liquor.

Something like the refrain--
one East-European national rag
or another, back in the heyday,
now trashed for two centuries--
on hold, strewn
over history's cutting floor.

His only refuge
beyond a litany of shelters
abandoned in resignation--
three-night stands
at most:

those tunes,
egging him onward,
alleyway to alleyway.

Tweetings from the Great Leader

Who fucking cares
where the storm was headed?
Alabama my peeps.

Always gotta stay on base.
No base, no party.
Bring it all down

to the comfort
zone. Let'em chill
in God and white
complexion.

Belligerence held
in reserve
'til I got there.
Bring it down.

Stay on top.
Who knows
how this will all end--

what with rivers over
run and storms
from nowhere?

But we know
who belongs on top,
who we want there.
Play your bass.

Not so bad
for the women—

Sheathed in beauty,
left with
consequences.

What is so wrong,
a little snatch?

They liked it too—mostly.
I am poetry,
not that you'd guess,

strip-mined
from the lodes
of resentment.
Power, luster, profit
gouged out
by the container
to tribal chants.

Crushed down, language
on the swift belt,
anthracite into glitter.

The taunting raspberry lingers--
complacencies of the golf-
course.

What the fuck
is empathy

anyway?

Atlas of Vanished Places

1.

I present you—
with this checklist,
register, transcript—
of places traversed.
They welcomed me
into their *khōra*, nurtured me—
in that manner of
receiving.

Crossed in an instant;
inhabited months long--
I was there. By what
engrained laws will
they persist?

Gone viral, a playlist,
an entire universe,
places accessed once with ease,
backlit cherished memory.
Walled off. In lock
down, verboten.

Awakened
into their overwrought
patchwork with a start. Always deepest
night. Always to the clatter of the 23 Trolley.
Tentative along the cobblestones, Chestnut Hill,
agonizing down Germantown into the City,
missing steep decline on right @ Mt. Pleasant. Sweeping
Memorial Lovett Library by . . . stupas, Angkor Wat ablaze, dawnlight
corona, neonatal sunbath--day, month, decade, millennium, eon . . .
Genova, lower city; only muted light filters down here—labyrinths--
stunted is what the Italians bequeathed to urbanity, nonetheless
leading . . . trattoria banal, recessed, unleashing
sonata in a vitello tonnato . . . edging toward Chelten,
the 23, once Center City rhizome, cine-mecca.
Orpheum! Bandbox! Past 18th c. manors, Schoolhouse
Lane. Rattling past Ashmead →Nicetown . . . entire glorious mountain,
Ladakh, chipped amethyst! Having staggered past kindred masses
turquoise, lapis-blue. . . . Phoenix Lounge, Ecke Kyffhäuser/Barbarossa,
tankards high above the terrace, floating Wagnerian servers . . .
46th/Queens: gastro-cornucopia: dried pear, olives, strudel, Parrot;
meze to die for, Sofra, Muglai Kebab; samosas, if called for--Cardamom . . .
Far East of Jackson Heights: Que Rico Taco!, 89th/Northern . . .
routinely surpassing eponymous expectation! . . . Greenspace,
34th/Junction, congregated families, lingering late weekend afternoon--
before the plague--solicitude, intimacy. Social isolation?
Endlessly patient 23 finally discharging, Washington Sq. morphing
into Rittenhouse, with a swing SW into 21st, old Gilded Cage,
coffee legend, plainly discernible, haunted, Odets,
orchestra musicians, shrine, Philly's tenuous claim,
lefty solidarity. Germantown Ave.
threading through it all.

3.

Hallowed, radiant,
enshrined—
tremulous altar,
my memory—
not yours, perhaps.
My sacred topoi.
This--their bill of lading.

Inaccessible
as my toothache--
Wittgenstein's
reckonings.

May they be blessed--
 all your places,
 my brothers & sisters
 of confinement,
all the odd corners,
fellow internees—

However you shunt them aside,
returning, again & again.
"Transitional objects" of the mind,
reserved, prized--
memory's display cases.

Exhausting pilgrimage.

Gaia rouses herself,
another tenuous round—
grappling--
the most recalcitrant herd
ever to emerge.

Co-lateral Dommages

To my brothers & sisters, Corona, Elmhurst,
fallen in earth not yet consecrated,
sanctity, à la Passchendaele,
Somme of battles, yet still our blood--
unconditionally.
However our Democracy, now rigged & perverted,
Democracy once proclaimed and blessed amid upheaval,
older brother to all of us toying,
contending with poetry.
elder sibling Walt & model.

1.

Reduced to plasma screen, unitary field,
what I'm allowed to engage with,
everything Real (& then some)--it all checks in.
Instantaneously: communiqués in earnest;
headlines issuing out of the remote steppes
of the collective unconscious;
benign wishes, tinged pornographic;
special deals, razorblades & mousetraps;
florentine scandals & sandals.
Case of emergency!

                                        A line

from nowhere alights, my spread
sheet: "MyExcess: Join the Survey.
U must tolerate cookies."

2.

Newly strewn, shallow graves, brothers,

sisters, Astoria, Bed-Stuy, long-awaiting you.
These the by-product, decades of feeding frenzy, omnivorous extraction,
goods, profits, with the power to subjugate, disenfranchise,
gilt-framed procedural impunity. Infinitely more sinister
than a firetruck, not entirely urgent,
U lavished on yr nephew; or the modest stockpile,
xtra undies U set aside.

                              Long

attenuated, sublimely sinister,
strip-mining the soul, an open pit,
discernment warped beyond revival.
Social contracts once thought weight-bearing girders,
detonated--by fiat.

                              Reasonable

expectations:
bio-political citizenship; public schooling,
in literate fundamentals.
Guaranteed protection, loose guns, looser shooters--
obliterated--
in a single news-cycle!

                              Revolution

by belligerence, exasperation; mass
lobotomy, express delivery, social media;
unchecked pronouncements rising in fugue,
delusional; involuted skeins,
double self-aggrandizing logic.
Insanity no crime in these U.S.

                    Negotiating capitalism's forbidding towers,
                              cruising the campus,
                    I stumble upon the hunting ground--
                              narcissist personality.
                    New character on the block.

                    Borderline. Abrupt swings:
        engrained insecurity→bizarre megalomania.

Revised format, subjectivity.
Leaping into flight, Birdman the model,
flip-outs umpteen x daily.
Character without character, driven, insatiable envy.
Man fitted out. Function: actor to role.
Perfect capitalist tool.

3.

Stately cargo ships, overladen,
bumper to bumper, identical,
fleet skirting Venice, negotiating lagoon.
Witnessed, backbay of Grand Canal, Spring '97.
Far, far too wide a berth
to shoehorn historical channels,
long-distance trade,
once upon a commodity--
when puny sails edged out these waters.
Tankers glide by, in silence,
thumb their prows in the nose of the modern city-state,
Venice—time-honored original!

Back

from oblivion, the Doges.
They rebound from the morgue,
superannuated political configurations,
in domination, thought safely archived,
in time's inaccessible warp.

Direct 2 U--

1215 AD. New Global Lords.
Zombie vestiges, medieval aristocracy,
Spectral reruns, history's horror-show,
cocktail of the depassé
mothballed in full brutality,
as flamboyantly posited--
Deleuze/Guattari,
Direct to you from Paris!

Montparnasse's
borschtbelt duo.

Any schmo
these days ingenious enuf--
to wield a tap, a sluice, a patent--whatever gauge,
to these SUBLIME flows,
strategic minerals, rare earth, what have you,
genius breakthroughs, deemed
INDISPENSABLE TO ADVANCED TECHNOLOGY—
lords in utter self-certainty,
under the hegemony of digital platforms.
Safely vaulted away, those ancient analog enforcers:
lance, pike, and ball-and-chain.

Wealth—
endlessly accruing--cash, shares, influence, bitcoin—
accounted, administered, multinational corporate ENTITIES,
bolting offshore, always.
Beholden less & less to anything deliberate,
say government, social agency, community.
And the payback—magnanimously bestowed--
always on prominent display, in the
museum, hospital lobby,
under the aegis of nobility's heraldic emblem--
philanthropy.

Epoch of the oilygark.
Heralding barbarism's eternal return.
Welcome back, Charlemagne!

4.

U count yr Honor yr distinction.
Tell me another.
Yr honor too drains Gaia,
Valyous U profess, levitating U
one nano standard deviation

beyond the swarm,
grasping, stampeding human folk—
desperate to distraction,
yr neighbors.

Honor
tilting yr screw poles,
whichever addiction yr personal mantra:
power, sex, $, getting high,
being pure, intimacy—
all virtual states, grandeur, expansion--
anchored in substances--
dependency's hollow cousins.

Honor--of
sexual probity, abstinence, transgression.
Of adultery, "marriage, true minds,"
honor, advanced degrees, logical acuity,
honor, drink: "Bottle cannot
kill him . . . head, bloodied but unbowed."
Yes, & "still captain of his soul" (Bateson channeling Henley).

Honor, vengeance on yr daughter's
dishonor, honor, being
white man, spreading carte blanche murder,
honor, proud gun owner.

Honor, imaginary suicide,
secreted, w vintage treasures,
at the rear extremity of yr closet—
breakwater, shame's abrupt tsunami.

"Give it up!"
Mr. K.
notoriously noted.

5.

All leading back→
Cycle of Reproduction—sacred mystery,
carnal joy & Spirit once cavorted,
imbued w species' fondest fantasies:
prolongation, creative mutation.
Midstream in glorious evolution,
the weave of our social fabric
endemically unraveled--

                  warping
women into opportunities,
some bonko twist on the Protestant Ethic,
laced with statistics, metrics of
productivity.

                  Urging on
seduction, college sport, cottage industry,
sexual tourism seeking offshore sites,
the best laid reservations.
These the carnal spoils, rewards—
service extraordinaire to multi-tiered
systems of accumulation,
tasks duly posted, spreadsheets summating years.

6.

Sidelined all, all in whispers from the wings,
pronouncements—issued in high alert,
from nothing less than a seer!

Hereby nominate myself—
prophet of pastrami,
scourge to the arteries,
dripping fat & peppercorns,
the lightning rod of human stupor,

rebounding from fatality's deepest
recesses & piled high—surrealist cloudbanks
in the sky.

In what canon
2 come or B
will this legend
B enshrined?

Geniza

Hearts of buckled parchment,
overladen & overwhelmed,
scribbled legends of ventures, travesties,
measured out in lifetimes,
frenzy, oblivion--shattered.
Sensibility's whimsical nerve
tissue, indelible, intractable
before the Law!

Who'd have anticipated the surge,
the deluge--of all
things, in paper!

                                        Each book,

pamphlet, printout
claiming an exclusive Cartesian
point in the archive of the mind,
each scrap screaming out
its singularity; the direst need
for its preservation. In the hold
where each memory capsule--
lived life freeze-dried--
springs to life once again!

                                        History,

folktale, even collective dream
secure in the Geniza! Each broadside,
torn and worn, more gauze than surface,
a fully naturalized citizen,
in the exilic community--
refugee texts.

Paper

storage crisis!
All cognitive freight jotted down,
fierce emotion trailing bills of lading.
The Law of Conservation
holding out no promises
to this accruing mass,

printed

matter & energy.

Script, contortion,
writhing up from every
leaf dragged forward,
ants en masse hoisting
with military bearing.

Birthday

cards scrawled, tremulous signage,
long-departed ones, faintest tracings.
Clippings, one family milestone or another--
We made it into newsprint
from the Philly hinterlands!

Tissue

paper relations, history
overbearing in trauma, despair.
How EVER banish,
discard, divest, expunge this
ramifying script fabric?
Out it billows from the

Geniza, Platonic Cave,

preserve of preserving,

for each new entry a stamped receipt.
Paid in Full: generation-dues.
Community, family belonging—
to a village of shared memory,
burden & remorse.

Notebooks, files, convolutes,
comics, wanton fantasies.

Borne by Stoics--
one immaterial repository
to the next.

Three Deer in a Development
near Harrisburg, PA

--Together, animals confer their powers of movement and perception on the biosphere, making it an organized collective, the largest organic being of all.

--Rather, the conversion to waste to a surplus by one life form has biospheric precedents: far from impoverishing the planet, the waste of one may, in fact, create more wealth for another.

—Lynn Margulis and Dorion Sagan, *What Is Life?*

1.

Sauntering forth possessed
cover of dusk—
family of deer

ranging over habitat
gouged free from meadows, high
ridge—

peopled, stately homes
verging on the French
provincial, buttressed--

low, restraining decks,
natural wood. Expanse
peppered, birdbaths

trolls, lawns
seldom fenced in. Elastic
ribbons, asphalt

slathered over greenspace.
Serried arbiters of order:
lamposts, curbside

property markers,
numbers. The deer
pay them no mind.

                                        2.

Only by force, kismet
do we drift—
SLOWLY
into one & same
crossing, paralytic
Augenblick,
eye to eye in
alien coordinates,
nuclear trio of deer
and I. Conducted--
network of ties—
community, decorum, family,
rules of the road
am I.

                                    They
follow the wind
roused by sunlight
out low-pressure troughs
gathering in clearings--
woods long ago having assumed cloaks,
inaccessible, inviolate. Volatile
winds flaunting all human compartments:
habitation, sovereignty, custom, habit,
turning any direction on a whisper or an acorn,
at nano-instant's notice; pulverizing the top-down
on grace alone--power, dominion
into smooth space.

                                        I and the deer

in our cabal, the biosphere;
they in fluidity, noble bearing,
we in God-given ingenuity
(major chimera). Ex-urban
housing developments:
Here we hold our parleys.
obscure, unattended.
High-end products,
both of us, the Bambis & I,
conversant in the tangle,
the still luxuriant margin,
tall as the troposphere, down
to volcanic rock
straining at the base,
warping continental shelves,
Antarctica—

Wherever protists roam,
bacteria prevail. Global managers
the deer & I,
Ivy-educated executors—
the "Life" account.

                                        3.

                                  High-tailing it

over broad communal lawn,
they couldn't give a flying
fuck, the deer. Disappeared,
with flippant coda!

Evolutionary
co-symbionts,
they fix us

with that uncanny
stare, Kafka's kitten-lamb—
egging us on—
slash them,
once and for all,
into oblivion.
We demur.

Too many
variables yet at play,
this slow-simmering ragout,

people and Gaia.

We'll long be gone the day
the deer lay down
their final say.

Ogre

All begins

civil faschion,
glass of chardonnay, profile
in the New Yorker.

Play

of manors: pointed civility
masking motives—strictly
lower echelon.
Avid extraction barrels
toward depletion.

The biz—

usual. Tales of woe
scrambled
into static,
biz into buzz
turned on low,
beyond thresholds
auditory
volume.

Og &

Magog, Biblical
extraction—familiar:
hirstute, monstrous
scale, menacing
gyration.
What we expect
from our

ogres—

voracious
groping graspers,

avid, avaricious.

                              Arctic fox,

lemmings, voles—
vanished.
Already in his maw,
save tails, pending
from the muzzle,
bloody stripes
dripping—through
gorypale
spittle.

                              Who

would ever suspect
successful
business
man, hewn
to the bottom
line?

                              Agog--

all attention!
Vertigo @ shifting
center, agora
reeling—endless
consumption, lousy
deals. Antagonistic
goner.

The Enchanted Isles

The always newborn
land drifted into forgetting.

                              The passed

vanished from the bridge
into mists too glad for the
swallow.

The future swept in like a wind
shaking the steel visor
riveted lately to the skull
to cement a ubiquitous
ceiling.

In the background
the still waters mumbled,
in languages still forgotten,
whose symbols
once overran the stamp
of huts and udders.

Presence spun out all over,

                              maddened

to be tripped in the timelock.
The guys went for 'cycles and stomping.
Trophies of Dixie on their bumpers.
Their tongues had a penchant
for jamming.

No strangers to wilderness,

their dreams. Nightly
converging over the aimless fields,
persistent clay upturned,
shattering the fragile dawn,
to tremors from ancient battles;
retreat, rear-guard,
from valor.

Class Notes

Secret behind the secret,
the all-unlocking detail—it could have sliced
thru the curtain of Maya, and with cleanth--
Had it only made itself known.

                                    Revealed, to be sure,

in the end. Only too late!
So is it always with inadmissible knowledge.
Fating Oedipus to take his fall—
No safety net to spare the trapeze-artist.
Welcome to nature!
(In its homo/femina sapiens brand).

                                    No oracles, seers

to warn us off the inevitable lives
of blunder, infelicity, bled
out in a cage, bars invisible, head battered,
rules unspoken, unspeakable gaffes,
insults allocated liberally,
recognized to no effect in hindsight,
oblivion systematic, the quiet unbearable--
a Love Canal interposing between
ourselves & our neighbors,
triggering a shared retreat into boggled silence,
muting the obvious inanities.
Shame!

                                    And subtending

all the comedies of manners--
the trampled park fences,
anointing footwear in dogshit--

prevails an even deeper system,
of selections, distributions—
O horror!

Determining

who grows up on landfill,
whose schools get staffed mostly by police,
who works, who sees the doctor—

I circulate through the nearby agora,
the adjacent boulevard bursting
with nano-encounters, chance only,
a twisted Möbius strip.
Bombarded by signals
raining from every direction.
Muscle cramps to the brain
from guessing their intent.
My fellow residents.
A neighborhood--suddenly
now an alien planet

Orbiting the stratosphere of chance human relations,
receiving, emitting messages randomly, out of control,
jamming personal radar waves.

To Nick Luhmann,

this is "double contingency"—
universal status of human encounter.
Terminal undecidability through mutual projection.
Transforming the street into a learning machine--
very antithesis of a tactical police tower.

Each new step

inciting error, misrecognition;
also a shot at squaring the skew.
Mending the Tissue of Life, shredded yet intact,

so long as we keep to our endless revision.

Yes, call me "Sir!"—

if you must. Unfathomable when this epithet
was first lobbed in my direction.
Veneration, my age? Everyday respect?
Ricochet, something overbearing,
my gait, my gaze?

"Sir!" as social distancing—

descended from that most venerable vocative order.
As you please, I accept!
Cordially, "Sir!"

I too, a pawn

like any other,
sold out to a hydra-headed system,
stuck, pressed hard against the pain of class,
each human situation an I Ching,
each unspoken boundary a hairline
tripped by inflection.

Catch it

in my stance, my voice—pitched--
my staccato prosody, emphatic sincerity,
my thankyous, my well-wishes.
Class by pronunciation, by education,
class by wristwatch, conspicuous consumption,
impeccable manners, by coverings,
concealed weaponry, by health-glow,
class by longevity.

Class plays bass

in race's brazen orchestration,
ethnicity's crafted lifestyles,
all dissonant, habit's grace-notes,
fine points drawn by religion--
polarizing filters held by the wielders of power
as they concentrate their sway &
swagger.

No worries—

class will keep you in grace,
holding you to your place; restraint constant.
No slipping thru electronic fences,
setting off sirens, armed defenses.

RACE IN YOUR FACE, but
CLASS UP YOUR ASS!

222

In Memory of Anthony Snively

Waning men,
meeting back again,
9/2014.

                                    50 years—

whether we fêted herd survival
or one another—
unclear.
                              Middlebrow hotel,

17th/Sansom, Center City.
Open buffet, cholesterol sinkhole.
Central HS, Philly.
Back then, no girls to shanghai
our thoughts or vital fluids.

                                  Iron filings,

drawn to our magnet school,
from every niche in the patchwork city.
Filing the halls, pursuing somber cycles
of core courses. Roster cards our taskmasters--
dictating the weeks that chained into months
in tin envelopes stamped out in metalshop.
Slide-rules peering out over chaos
from overburdened shirt pockets,
side-by-side with our boilerplate
routines.

                              Dissolving boundaries

any sort, became our chief diversion:
between classes, galvanized
into a Marlboro-puffing mass
strewn over the South Lawn,
our own minority, a republic

of mirth. Difference itself—
angle of a hat, nano-lull in
gait, pitch, accent--
the spark detonating levity.

I thumb--

the proverbial criminal returning--
through the pages, "Emphasis," Yearbook 1964,
rogue's gallery of demographics as of faces,
CHS 222nd class. A rhapsody mostly in white—
the color-wheel jammed back in those days.

Blooming

ethnographic encyclopedia--
captioned faces, mostly hopeful.
Among Irishmen, Jews, Italians, U.S. German
descendants in profusion--
rarer specimens of the Caucasian persuasion:
Ukrainians, above all; Hungarians, Armenians,
Scandinavians, the odd Latino—even a
meandering Puritan.
Our Japanese-American in solitary. In the place of
Iranians, Vietnamese, Haitians, Somalis,
East & South Asians—blank space.

Sunday brunch—

colonial market by Society Hill.
Tanking up on caffeine. Optional
for survivors of Friday's drinks,
testimonials, cream sauces.

Our Black brothers'

reminiscences ever so slightly in a different key,
HS business concluded, entrée, to *grandes écoles*
and some not quite, bankrolled, more often than not,
by athletic ability. On to lifetimes of valor—
yet by some baffling calculus ironclad
nonetheless, destined to utility--infrastructure,
security, vicissitudes of small business.

Progeny

of a decorous colonial city,
by the '50's it had morphed—
now a volatile nomadic zone--
hordes migrating from one district,
post-War Air 'n Light homes to the next.
Vast rowhouse tracts
abandoned in full White Flight--
all our classmates' families
registering this history.

Emerging

from one common special school
into wildly skewed systems of preference,
in some, advancement foreclosed.
From our shared database--schoolboy memory—
divergent lives, impossible to syncopate.

Back on the street,

all I'm being asked--
courteous respect, on equality's open plane—
not benevolence, even cordiality—
simple acknowledgment does it all.

Baseline dignity

not claimed but taken. This
our latest revolution.
One Spring afternoon, 2020,
the bottom fell out,
for anyone with the eyes to see, on
the U.S. futures market in
decency.

As to the studied amenities--
"smiling public" whitemen—
forget it!

Class of 1968

It was the jovial cardiologist,
healer, countless broken hearts
& vesicles—got it right & in a hand
shake's stroke: "You may mistake
the body or the face;
no sooner does the voice enunciate—
you've got the person, old soul,
whole deal, present & accounted.

Spasm of the pericardium,
downward tug of Time,
descending the abyss of the chest
into the abdomen, yes,
this is what Time is: passages.
In an instant taking in
more than could be ever
counted, tabulated.
Still no bowing back,
no retro eddies to that flow.

Loss--is all that time regains,
heart-subduing loss
in smiles, moods, places,
whatever moments, bodies
savors, have not yet slipped
memory's tenuous precarity
within the overbearing
tapestry of its traces.

On the far
shore of the psyclone—
an outstretched hand--
deliverance, survival.
We who had together persisted,

together apart, somehow
outlived, somehow outsmarted
lassitude, insouciance, burnout,
rage.

                              There
we were—cuddling together
on the shoal of survival,
by whatever vehicles
had delivered us,
we held on,
the business of living--
suspended.

Welcome—
to the taught pavilions
of reminiscence.
Casually distributed
among provisional tables,
we decanted old narrative,
bottled up vintage,
uncontainable in essence,
gathering one more
Time.

À une passante

1.

Into my aroused
surround you--

howls of need
utter in

dream already
familiar
all "reality
principle"

outrage
suspend
limit, horizon—

flapping strips,
stage
curtain.

Copper-buckled
mane, bowing,
plays me
in the sign
waves, oscillation
evidence,
your flesh.
Invitation,
to the voyage . . .

2.

Heartfelt
thanks deep image
engrained
my mind.

Forever.

                                    I thank you
and bless—
all, truly
I can do—

For your proud
bearing—you face
another day, another
mass, tangled

uncertainties, for
the lift, rising
up your ankles,
bones,
in smile—
random thought,
unexpected text.

                                    I take you in,
a wonder
a trance.

Thank you

far more than you
move—
gets you from place
to place

quicker than a camera
shutter, as you hunker
back to reading

skin, embroidery,
your nerves,
harboring
mysteries

beauty
far more
this panning
glance

however
impacted,
nocturnal
harvest

.

In sequence
I shuffle
out the sub
way carriage--
head bowed

Berlin

This habit of collecting cities,
it's getting to feel old shoe.
In a universe of cosmic
flow, diffusion, what,
after all, is another city?

Is it the storied constellation—
energies, bearings, precious sites--
hovering only over this place
or that, a dirigible flaunting
a brand name and a signature
for one urban habitat?

Nothing more than a crazed fly,
trapped between opposed,
parallel facets of the planetary
thoroughfare, buzzing,
endlessly banging
my fuzzy head between
radiant window pains--

My ultimate riddle--
of cities not of sphynxes--
why do I circle back?
Each lifetime berg,
a semi-precious stone,
strung along the choker of experience,
each one a counterlife—
I couldn't quite manage
coaxing it into Being--
too many the details.

The New Berlin accrues
before my eyes, each

postmodern construction--
tradition simplified
into a hieroglyph.

                French embassy—

its pristine lines
still resolve into shutters and balconies
though in a different universe
from grands boulevards.

                New Deutsche Bank.

Mere steps away from Checkpoint Charlie,
Masonic temple to sublime
investment. Invisible
billions now warehoused
along a global promenade
of bourses.

                Friedrichstraße.

Whores roamed here back then.
Up in the barracks
G.I.s sucked Panama Red
as they lined up the best
deals at the PX.

                Kudamm:

more stately than ever,
yet eklippsed
as entertainment nexus,
outshown--

                Now it's Potsdamer Platz!

Towers of open glass, neon,
surmounted by a planetarium
of LED searchlights, architecture

impervious to daytime doings,
only the cosmopolitan in its sights,
permanent night in the global city
always angling for boundlessness,
biznesses. Here the planners
opened out the agora--installing
colossal cinematographic windows.
Pervasive public phantasms
for not-so-private lives.

On the Death of P.S.

November 9, 1971

Devowered by forward and after
        word, the fed-up took a dip in the sign
                with no appetite, the
                      always-full water

and took his time.

                The last victim . . . of the War,
                caught up in the family
                loop, system
                closed & twisting back--
                again upon again, again^2--
                to the intransigence of
                suffering compounded by pain--
                its addictive allure.
                The exquisite reader,
                rewarding attentiveness
                far beyond the ransom
                it extorted . . . now
                & ever *immer* in the
                waters of the Halensee,
                Westberlin.

                          There

awaiting
the magnanimous gesture—
so grand when it honeys from the fingers of the last good man in Sodom &
                      Gomorrah,

it liquidates

                all former indignities.

And he was just back from
                Jerusalem.

                Beware your students; issues
                they have, clad in
                cloying sanity,
                they learn in teeth, gnawing
                through the final umbilical
                traces—AND

                your father,
                          unless Abraham.

You can never know he
                in the duplicity of fathering

                        wills you live.

Genocide

Phnom Penh: it is a tumble
down, no clear descent, what came before.
Open pit, festering streets, unhealed sore.
Demons fill the air, unchained
from Ramayana friezes scoring Angkor Wat:
only the deities can rein them in.

                              The specters of the dead—

resilient, ingenious. They've pitched their tents
in the set foreheads, the blank gazes
of the current residents, survivors—
anyone old enough to remember. However civil,
ceremonial the occasion, dark blood,
excruciating memory, haunt their faces.
Lingering traces, punishment en masse,
the tattoo of bamboo batons never abated.

                              Tassed by category,

the skulls rise in columns--
this the open-air Stupa of the Killing Fields--
in plexiglass cylinders,
form and transparency courtesy of history,
a testament to battered lives, to human remains
relegated to shallow pits all over.

                              You do not

enter this memorial without a tête-à-tête
with all the assembled poor Yoricks,
anonymous souls accumulating to sublimity.
You sidle by as you might a Yoni stone,

blocking the corridor among the ruins
of a nearby Hindu temple. No room to spare.
You stare, the exquisite rubble
persisting as monument to becoming-death:
rampant, endemic, wide as a whole society
in frenzy.

Is it for reassurance we've sought out these cranial reminders?
Animated icons of faciality, hard-wired
into human cognition, their ghostly gaze
sweeping, piercing you. But caught you they have—
staring. Nauseated by barbarism,
your prurient interest only further proclaims
your utter irrelevance.

Angkor Wat tourism--
it's going to reach 400,000 this year,
the official tells you. With an economy
hard at work on infrastructure--
1,000,000 before long. This is how
a land—having sustained a 3 ½ year regression
into anomie—builds tourism.
With an added touch,
crafts assembled by mutilés de guerre.

Over carvings of Angkor Wat
scripted reality reigns,
courtesy Ramakien. Brahma, Vishnu, Indra, and Shiva
dominate lintels, coding sacred precincts,
their images explicit, transparent.
Finitude in dimension and carving—
the substantive issue prevailing over Angkor Wat,
a humble portal to something vastly greater.
A scale model rendition: universe of gods, cosmic
forces unleashed in war and love,
Khmer culture at its crowning moment,
effulgence stretching toward every horizon--
while the West still adrift in its "Dark Ages."

Algebra the portal to the sublime in Indian religion--
so Leo Bronstein argued,
as deities & their limbs, endlessly repeated,
cascade to infinity. Each vast frieze a scene,
resolving in one archetypal worldly figure
two opposing life-forces in stalemate & apotheosis.
A universe suffused by cosmic tension
pulsating in waves or cycles--
while sacred texts spin out their variants,
singing in energia, dynamis, eros, karma—

The drive prodigious, incorrigible as jungle vegetation,
like the allure of dancing Apsaras.
Milky figures affixed to the wall
annotate a universe engendered,
bellicose rage & resolute seduction
nonetheless susceptible, checks and balances
restrained—gridlock in the cosmos.

Textures of Cambodia
more pitted than ever.
Never to be overlooked: temple of Neak Pean,
cistern in triumphant disguise as naga,
model for the trenches at every turn.
Through sinuous deviation, a mythic beast
detains the rainy season.

Incursions of the Real

The wailing of the sirens will not stop,
and the hordes barreling down West Avenue
toward the Battery, as the ambulances,
heading opposite, toward the cata
strophe, pile up, first to arrive.
Their drivers soon to find death,
vastly irregular numbers. We still scan
the harbor, with its commodious expanse
and its monuments to immigration,
multicultural latitude, for
more airplanes like the second, the one over
droning us with sickening staccato
as it plows into the tower,
whose flames still bound up with solar intensity
when we squeeze into the corner by the living-room window,
transforming the upper zones
of a soaring construction
into holocaust.

We now have a better idea
what composed the endlessly disseminating shroud
of smoke that drifted southward the first few days.
It was a dust event; dust whose finitude
matched its inertness blanketed
the city and its surrounding waters
from first impact—
metal, construction materials, human bodies—
pulverized into off-white by
product of sameness. The dust
still settles, drifting stiffly down,
barely material. It blanches the sidewalk
as a young woman, in tow to a white poodle,
saunters by. Early December still
a season away.

The torture, visceral as imaginary,
still hovers in the air, unresolved.
No cleanup act yet
delivers forgetting.
No brash narrative
steps forward to organize
the monumental happening:
into a Before & After, epochal
transfer, lightening
change of guard & open
breach in childhood
oblivion to the Real--
forever.

Twin projections of our global economy
earmarked by their soaring statement;
encrypted vulnerabilities deep
wired within the systems
of aviation and containment
(nuclear, biological, chemical)--
demanding to be taken at their word.
Vehicles of pleasure as of serious pursuit
transformed into lethal weapons;
swerves of the market written
into the script. With more
worldliness than we dared concede,
the system's foes read it meticulously,
glossing against the long grain
of its meander.

Kaleidoscopic jerking of the Real.
Its base-position:
complacent acclimation,
instilled normality. In a stroke,
& from the perch
of a TV divan,
the inconceivable
was passé.

And once during the agonizing interregnum,
before the towers go down in shock
& conflagration, a shower of panels
floats earthward from the celestial strata.
Leisurely, they surf
breeze and gravity. If I could only
capture the poems encrypted
on their facets!

Why should our metropolises and boroughs stand unscathed
by that distinctive tonus of chaos and indirection
settling in when population queers population,
when the consensus of mutual equanimity
devolves into systematic hostility? After
Cambodia and Rwanda, Belfast, Sarajevo, even
Jerusalem, why should the US of A
insist on a pristine transcript, cartoon mascots
to embellish the scene of sublime undermining, primordial
rivalry, heaving a pointed elbow in the gut,
life's by no means disinterested
momentum?

Yet Another Crime Mini-Series

Negotiating a skein,
tortuous crime-scene tape,
with low-heeled aplomb--
order resumes in the carbon-lit post-mortem tent,
hermetically zipped, barring contingency,
HAZMAT spacesuits de rigeur.
A solicitous pathologist presides
over a corpse mauled to the limit--
no doubt as to who or what
commands center stage.

The Commish is here!
Careworn, still fuckable,
the cowl of *Sorge* over her visage
confers authority.
Flesh resilient, hair understated.

Not so our corpse.
Dismembered, current ceiling on gory;
bizarre markings on the torso,
unspeakable plastic protrusions.

Donning surgical gloves,
from time-to-time prodding;
curt queries in a discreet undertone to the attending doc;
detectives standing by for orders.

Formalities concluded,
Commish hazards a working prognosis.
Unmistakable work before us:
psychopathic serial-killer--
first magnitude.

Back at the station, only
subterfuge, humiliation. Summarily
removed from the investigation!
Unwittingly she's stumbled into a multi-crime tangle.
Open latticework, ingenious murders,
regional repercussions, reaching high up—
maybe even the Minister.
Her officious male superior
takes all necessary precautions--
X'ing her from the picture.
From the Examining Magistrate
who might intervene, only mixed signals.

On the domestic front, only slow torture.
Awaited at home perpetually,
troubled teenager: internet porn, drugs,
all the wrong parties.
Commish single mom, natürlich!
Barely one step ahead, Protective Services.
Mr. Ex surfaces, periodically--
sorely needed quickie.
SO wrong!

When will she melt? we wonder. With whom?
Here too we uncover suspects in multiple,
serially cancelling each other out--
NEVER with her sidekick & cruiser partner—
affable, impeccable, married.

Men these days, not in the strongest position
to sustain public confidence. They harbor
weird conceptions as they tender
distaff colleagues with on-job training.
Invariably a lady, our Commish,
As she updates a wide swathe of jurisdictions.
sensible head to toe—now reaching
from Iceland to Turkey, Australia
thrown in. Likelier to settle
an impenetrable cold case in Antarctica than
unearth an uncompromised male official.

It is the little screen we delegate,
all by way of distraction,
to right grave injustice,
chilling trends & propensities--
to stave off pending catastrophe.
With a familiar cast of characters—
our partners in delay, evasion;
innocuous co-conspirators,
ominous inaction.

Fade

Articulation in the manifold of seeing,
the rhythm-break at the heart of heartbeat's go.
Artfully installed, precision-timed fadeouts
hold the pose, crown the vignette,
unfurl the still until almost unbearable,
underscoring a cliché in aura, a retard
in a multiplex symphony, with
digressions & subtitles—

                    In full splendor,

the fadeout beckons:
rousing us from the dogged rhythm,
the predictable flow--rupturing
the splice-induced Time-Image.

                    The Silents—

singing Sirens,
beguiling our imagination with fatal attraction
the older they get. Luring
sensibility beyond the brink of disaster—
launching a cavalcade of images in a crash palace.

                    The fade--

disheveling the rhythm of spectacle
into a staccato of fits and starts,
shredding my nerves in a sudden enigma:
flashy flourishes trailing off into meek diminuendo.
Montage at a tango's tempo,
cued to dream's unhinged logic.
Intrusive traffic light, mid-flow
in a sequential art form,

agent of forgetting, obfuscation--
cinema's most guarded secret.

                    Enough

to transform Marlene Dietrich into a kitten!

                    & when the Real

impinges itself upon this medium—above all,
one of collective imaginary projection,

                    importing

the unmistakable fungal whiff of death itself,
simulating blood and gore through time-honored cine-alchemy,
bringing us face to face with precisely those eventualities
we struggle not to contemplate,

those affirming—conclusively—the out of control--

whether as lurid automobile accident,
the torments of death as drawn out in a Goya engraving,
or a pill-induced medical emergency--

                    ALWAYS

have we been visited, stroked--
fadeout's faint caress.

                    [Spontaneous after
                    shadow.]

Halloween

For E. E.-H.

At the level of true knowledge,
I have stuffed human corpses,
several of them, beneath the floor
boards of a residence in Buffalo, NY,
proceeding undeterred through the years
as teacher, father, spouse acknowledged
by the community. While searches
for these lost neighbors proceeded,
evidence mounting, never quite leading
to my doorstep—deeds overshadowed--
in the overarching struggle
for sustenance, recognition, cognizance,
camouflaging not only me—but
those who might discern my crimes as well--
all caught up in the gaudy Halloween
of civility.

On a commodious

loop of lawns, set slightly off--
last one in—the dwelling persists,
decorous, expansive, retiring.

While I assess damages

perpetrated by myself, no other,
upon a pliant, stability-seeking ecosystem.
What renewal let alone forgiveness might ensue?
Care, attentiveness, patient instruction—
all squandered?

Extract--

harshly from the environment.
It is my nature.

Food, pleasure, relaxation—

more from duty than any exertion—
I lay my hands on these commodities
fast as I can wrench them out,
from Terra's planetary womb:
trifles of the delicatessen,
chip-driven toys, goldfoil & plastic—
these the media prevailing
within my ever-receding polis.
Fantasy and game designed by genius
to recharge, even in nano-segments.

What give, allowance remains,

within an entrenched system—
bullheaded self-aggrandizement, venality raised to religion,
impenetrable interlocking buttresses
reifying what was only yesterday
indented under madness,
marching in columns
in diagnostic manuals?

Deliver unto me please,

in time's excruciating slow drip—
any stay, recess, relaxation, whatever,
even slightest reprieve,
to be brokered at the stillest
of all hours.

As ever

shielded by masonite pegboard,

dripping with dust & tools,
powered by electric.

                    I tinker on.

Secure. My private Unabomber's cabin.
Do-it-myself. Editing,
shredding, expunging former disguises.

What is Called Thinking

The night heaves around me, a precipitous stomach virus.
Thrown randomly among the swells, my bedlinens,
night endures; blessing of sleep
falls upon the wardens, quieter souls,
graced with some modicum of humility.
I do know better.

Once again has my private language
gotten the worst of me.
One more time--
no runnels for the runoff;
night the ultimate receptacle, *khōra*.
On it goes,
sweeping mercurial children along
for the roller coaster.

Should know better; I err.
The wrong situations
drape lax arms over my shoulder,
crushing with familiarity.
Fault lies with the disaster movies,
primal scenes, they coax me
into their soap-plots,
having their way.

As this night lurches onward
in its utter indiscretion,
unwelcome guest,
the one who forgot to bid farewell,
it is the "banality of evil" who insinuates itself,
uninvited company.

It would approach overstatement
to venerate thinking as calling;

it is rather, the demand
by an impervious lover to turn over,
on pain of exposure—
sins of lust, gartersnake variety,
husbanded at the garden's tropical
corners, zones despoiled the most
by greenhouse exhalations.

Thinking as terminal indigestion.
The night pukes us out squirming,
legs spinning toward crevasses in the wall-paper;
rumination foisted upon us--
all else has devolved into cancellation.
The interminable sentence:
It is.

Dead Birds

A conspiracy of dead
birds--following me, where
ever.

Caught
between the labia
of a grandiose
marble monument, we
saw three together.

"It's a curse," you shuddered.
"I don't know on who."

They have been
true since that day, while
I have trafficked with a mob
of cities. Always color
less, the way birds who die
in cities are, they lie
often beneath power
lines & in the
shadow of utility
poles. Once

I might have reasoned,
'Birds have to fall
somewhere, why not here?'
They themselves are signs.
What they have borne
far more than curse,
beyond all gesture.
They know.

A

out out
somewhere
west of Meridian
but north of Spain

a sick letter is puking its guts
out against the
sky, heaving.

It would be impossible to tell
for sure whether an A or D

for the poor bastard's stomach
scrawl's collapsed,
leaving him all but
trenchant.

It was no use, said the
foundations.

out out poured
all the stuff we know
to be on the insides of
things,

fluids and pastes,
dark shapeless growths
packed in frills of
membrane

out out they empty, in spasms,
imitating the sea,
released

through the lassitude of diseased
organs. Is alcohol
the root of this
sickness?

All running from the
space

there is no cross or loop
to contain, no hope
to penetrate.
out out

Crakow

Well-

come by those wise Yur

Peons, of a Some

Day PM down in the Entral

Square, not nessa

serially Recht

angular, streets

fanning everywhichway, fabric

of lives opened, sea zoned, ex

panded all pistes

wind down 2 the Sq on Sum

day.

uncouth Mur

kins putting in

command performance,

GOTTA be there. Me

right among'm more

cities, times, seasons

than I care to wreck in,

Aix, Exeter, Xian, Antwerp, Barcelona,

Prague, Florence, Basel,

Toulouse, trapped, Renault 5, nother ur

bane labrinth! latest Crakow

dunnim' all, safely in

cognito, no

body 2 reckon old accounts with,

nobody 2 call. Pro

fected in fashion,

soshall insulation, movement

my cocoon, my ad

dress, jetlag.

Shock Potatoes

Dispatches hailing from the tenuous screen,
I am their subservient prophet.
Polaroids of trauma flashing up,
whether on LED or plasma--
in shards slivering the eye,
always at an oblique angle, sharpening,
were it possible, the sting and
accumulated pain.

This is the beating we keep taking
day in day out again, a pummeling
on the TV couch, even with its rounded cushions.
Or on the clinical Steelcase chair.
Taken amid comfort--drinks, snacks in profusion.

Beatings for certain—
nonetheless.

                                        Planetary

soap operas, themes predictable--
hunger, sweat, aggression and retreat,
death and entropy.

                                        Spare

me details, the yet further disheartening facts,
well-known well in advance, boredom stupendous,
peeling off turbulence, its reeling bobbin undone at the fringes,
whispering in the dialect of strange attraction.

                                        The newsreel,

meandering in a Möbius strip, twisting
while it unwinds, successfully eludes
all efforts at editing, expurgation.

Scandals

in all seasons, vying in ingenuity,
two flavors, only:
sexual incontinence or sticky fingers.
Suicide notes posted in full view:
public servants pushed to their own annihilation, unable
to sustain the severe ultimatum.

Shocking the body

politic, in its aimless roller derby,
its untethered gladiators tilting at the brink of oblivion,
craved for exposure, any form or medium,
elbowing all obstacles into the gutter,
barring no holds or perfidy--
Their attorneys, deputies of habituation,
coaches in outlandish fabrication--
always on standby.

Out on the open sea

why, there's Connecticut! Or is it Rhode Island?—
Antarctica in state-sized chunks divesting
of its continental shelf in mad abandon,
reducing to an oceanic bouillabaisse.

While yet

unseen by human eye,
those opportunistic VIRUSES
slam in tidal waves into our villages and habitations,
mutating faster than we, locking us down,
demoting us into prey.

                                        Spare me, please—

those rogue celebrities,
spurious public personae inveighing every imaginable topos,
toxic tongues gagging. Intransigent media
lording over tribal encampments.
What count as communities sequestered to custom e-hives;
loudest buttons on the band,
droning forth in personal-pan invective.

                                        A public

of predators and targets: estranged
to the reaches of utter non-recognition,
living off identical RNA! While we,
marauding bear removed by force
from the town dump, baited by goads in overload,
stung at every extremity—

                                        Careening

about the cage,
mania past tipping point
(half-heartedly, we hazarded what we could in circumspect--
only after the pantomime of civility
had devolved into universal
thrashing).

                                        In restraints

for our own good,
we strain at the traces toward the dump--
where with impunity, we deposited
voided electronics, cans, crates
good for eternity.

Visits to Hometowns Never Inhabited

Yes, you do turn back—
back, back, back, you wander
down trails denuded of markers, signposts.
Provinces of an alien land;
tracks with their meanings effaced, defaced—
maps, mappings absolute.

Yet here you are--immersed
in an entire region of unknown cities,
bewildered—shuttling from point to point,
utterly disoriented, locale to locale.
Their being no palpable reason to be here--
save one.

Caught! Bouleversé: once again—
by an overwhelming surge
of memory and desire, in reverse.
A flood of resurgence,
second-hand memories under toe.
Undertowed, deeper & deeper,
by abandoned cities,
stations in a family quest,
a propre Odyssée—translated—
over obscure decades,
into idiome privé.

Off a stately boulevard,
synagogue, Cluj: continuous use,
despite the intervening generations,
multivalent political upheaval.
Soaring double Moorish spires,
anchors of solidity, crowned
by tentative onion cupolas.
Between the towers,

a prominent Magen David in stained glass
delivers a strong message.

                             In awe at the discovery

of a steppingstone in a lost family history,
at least a possible one,
I imagine my Grandpa
David Louis Glickman, unseen & unmet,
d. 1933, Lewistown, PA,
on some occasion fixing this place
between the eyes, perhaps enroute→
Pittsburgh, 1890.

My direct male forebear on the maternal side,
relegated to the Imaginary by circumstance,
just couldn't handle the city. Pursuing
the jagged trajectory of the peripatetic peddler,
heading E from Pittsburgh and demanding
the comfort of his fellow chanting Jews,
he dragged my Grandma and a gaggle of girls
(a missing chromosome story, we believe)
through a string of Pennsy towns,
each with a Shul and a minyan.

Past lives unlived and only imagined.
Here I am in Cluj, returned in the purely hypothetical,
to snap this house or another,
snap, snap, as I've snapped countless,
arrayed on a diasporic chain: Allegheny, Ford City,
drawn backward, wandering in lust and submission,
along the immemorial Way. Stations
on the trail of love, the only true highway,
driven, for lack of a better phrase,
by the great outpouring.

Snap, snap.
I've snapped towns as they've survived--
ancestral houses & homes in potentia,

placeholders really, for projections
allowed to subsist in the void,
popup memories ratified post facto.
Loggy I've tramped myself,
long drives, expensive flights, even to Cluj—
snapping, divining for any tap on LOVE—
open-ended, unconditional,
onceuponatime.

Snap snap. Cities, in stately panorama, imaginary—
in each heady cocktail of solace,
crushing isolation.

Love in insufficiency.
It all comes down to that,
condensed to just a couple of messages—
the Greeks knew all about it—
cryptic, clipped to the bone—
flashes of the Real.
Micro messages affixed to bleached signposts,
thunderclap mantras,
just one or two of them--it all comes to that--
and the Road, the "I" prized open,
whatever the cost.

                    The inexhaustible journey—

it all comes down to knotted muscle,
reading the signs.

Where U R

1.

If U only but knew where U are,
where U were, where U might be,
instead of this floating, we call it "surfing" now.
Commonplaces of the electron,
in constant pirouette between,
between messages, (how many of consequence?)
Between signals, imperatives, yous—

U might be free.
Are you?

FAR out on the land,
space-sweep of the breakaway continent,
c. 96,000,000 BC, land
FARFAR OUT, utterly parched red clay,
upsurge of water the rarest indissecretion,
boulders, rocks, projections,
deep-fissured earth the substrate;
foreground of reds, mauves, browns,
at the singed register of the rainbow,
plodding into a horizon issuing forth
to those who dared presume a way of life
within its compass—never to arrive.

NOTHING more imperative
to the uncompromising, resolute indwellers,
this inhospitable, unspeakably gorgeous place,
nightmare case to the etiquettes of geography:
knowing where they are.

2.

Wandering in, on a sunstruck,
lightstruck Sunday AM, April, awash--
sky opal-blue, inconceivably wide & open,
blessed Sydney lawns—magpie, ibis, cockatoo
layover, even glorious rainbow lerikeets swarming!
Amid stands & patches: scentless rosewood,
leaved paperbark, wattle, needlebush.

Sunday in a different park!
Solicitous repose, commodious lawn, urbane green tide,
eye of the hurricane held at bay.
Great Antipodal Port's business district,
up from the Rocks & Circular Quay!

GRACIOUS

Sydney, portaged away from Botany Bay,
beacon & depot, monitor & storehouse,
sublime global flows!

Coal, metals,

rare earth, CUMODDITIES—
furious output, those Asian TIGERS
(random monGOOSE thrown in)—
computers, appliances, clothes, cars,
capital itself in humungous batches,
serried flotillas, overstuffed super-
barges, plying stately the coast,
Melbourne to Sydney, beyond—

Violently extracted things

VALUE ON BOARD!
Expropriated from the hides of gangs,
repatriated village-people jammed together,

endless work bench, ballroom-sized maquiladora,
while the intemperate towers—NEO-MANHATTAN--
sprout-up all around them,
bankrolled, Commonwealthbank!
Products of land, forest & sea,
seized in tropical haste & fecundity
by agribusiness.

Antipodal global portal posing--
as a lapsed vegetarian brazen in non-repentance.
Torn from Terra herself,
parched, pitted, furrowed, vastly overextended,
undernurtured & sub-husbanded.

                  With the City heated up,

far beyond control, caution, or contrition,
accelerated to frenzy, by all this congress.

                  Beneath

preening-proud towers
for record-keeping, securities, banking,
crowds throng beleaguered streets
questing beer & entertainment.
While rents soar, consumer goods morph
into treasures, exiling
all but most established, entrenched—the managers--
back out to the hinterland,
FARFAR away. Almost all the way
to the aboriginal homelands
where in some mythical time,
the entire cycle of making, exchange, and using
wrenched itself from equilibrium.

3.

Once again drawn,

brilliant April P.M. in Sydney,
down to national jewelry box, (Art Gallery, NSW).
Dreams, memories, ghosts,
most recalcitrant obsessions.

Set in Victorian probity

on the lawn, the Domain.
Between Greek columns—themselves overwritten,
legends: the Greats, Aeschylus to Donatello.
You enter a cube, a remnant--
from the Great Modern Age of Museum Construction—
soon resolving into a glass-steel
downward sweeping slope, late XXc. vintage,
opening its panorama over the always buzzing Bay,
the ultimate in bay windows!

Here enshrined,

treasures of the Aboriginal,
deterritorialized denizens of the land,
relocated, now, as ever—
artists—of place, flow, energy,
memory.

And what panels

they bestow upon the nation-state
of their dispossession!
Roadmaps of what came before,
what might persist below,
inchoate forcefields throbbing
@ the seismic foundations,
still setting a floating continent,

eons since its breakaway,
off on the loops of its ricorsi.

Business acumen

not likely the defining skill
of these painters: in payment
for their forced marginality they offer,
wrested back from erasure, topography--
tenuous palimpsests reserved
only for the eyes of the
most resolute observers &
most patient readers.

Flooded by light.

Crowds of a Sunday,
demanding impunity to see;
scanning for images in flight, flashes,
who they might be.

4.

If this all could even suggest

a frame, "Warlugulong,"
Clifford Possum Tjapaltjarri, Tim Leura Tjapaltjarri (1976).
Field of fields in multi-focus, each intricate sector
blurring and blurred by the neighbors,
footprints dancing unconstrained over tapestry;
the occasional interposed arrow
interjecting a direction.
However disoriented this terrain,
it sustains a land for the living.

Bisected

by roads themselves converging--
canvas as map, the Territory—

zones inhabited by monads in gradations of intensity,
with color the medium of distribution,
strewing the ground with grades:
of passion, submission, indifference.

                                    Soul itself

glides over the aerial flowchart--
the mood: psychic expenditure and absorption--
knowing what to expect in each locality:
forming orderly neighborhoods of attention,
bounded--clouds, forests, streams.
No whimsical dream this strong composition.
Orienting an entire spiritual community—
to the Central Flame, the Animating Campfire,
the First Principle, raging & devouring--
the act of founding.

                                    Resplendent!

Containing, delivering the unexpurgated miracle—
turbulent space!

Nothing stable left on this map,
zones, climates, sensibilities in constant torment,
yet painting is home--not only to Tjapaltjarris,
long-steeped in hospitality—
but to all.

                                    This the only

homeland we might hope for;
habitation--at stake in this conjuring,
this literature of habitation, scene,
the *khōra* of persistence,
since time's emergence,
writing insinuated itself
everywhere, for all time, whatever
we might happen to be.

                                    Rhizomes

of indwelling—concentrations of energy
counter-intuitive in their visual balance,
the marked rationality of their design,
their economy of form.

To this alternate world

Uta Uta Tjangala issues the empowering invitation,
"Untitled (Jupiter Well to Tjukula)" (1979).
Map of mapping, connections,
one zone of intensity to the next—
seamless (if angular). Plunking
us down in the midst of an imaginary homeland,
intercourse between all its hubs,
an understated rationality
pervades this invisible city.

Entranced!

Rare harmony of palette
(browns, greens, yellows in powerful balance),
we gladly seek admission to this virtual polis--
for its civility.

Gliding

above the only scape that matters,
of states & moods & colorations & rhythms,
of sea-changes in temperament and sensibility.
Ports of call in "Aboriginal painting's" guided
journey: "intensities" in the patois
of the immortal Spinoza, Nietzsche, Deleuze & Guattari—

Not entirely

outré, this canvas, with its tri-plane--
3 stacked propellers,
spinning out of a mandala luscious pink to the core.

"Water & Wallaby Dreaming,"
Dick Pantimatus Tjupurrula (1981).
Aviation invoked here, on every plane,
animating the vision.

                              Far below,

a carpet of densewoven flowers chants:
disorienting melody, beneath a floral tapestry.
The wallaby of legend peers out the foliage;
circular settlements nestle amid the coils of a stream;
birds shadow the airplane colonizing the sky.
In a rare harmony of form and movement, color and mood,
a dream enunciates itself as floral effusion.
Far-flung settlements, circles & spirals,
infiltrate the weave of this
scripted geometry.

                              Habitation--

at the very crux of these paintings!
No postal address situates or demarcates this zone.
Rather, Way of Being, a slant,
bearing, a line of flight, burst of thought.
These dominate the topography of outback--
unremitting luminosity by far
its prominent feature.

                              5.

If you only knew where you might stand in your own dream,
a tissue of screen memories,
whether of the group or your own twisted path.

                              This is the place

of the tropics, icons, semes
furnishing any semblance of your significance;

if you only knew into which thicket,
which system of sluices, waterholes, campgrounds
the incontrovertible facts drew--

If U only knew
where you are!

Henry Sussman is a critic and writer currently living in New York City. Trained in nineteenth and twentieth-century Euro-American Literatures and Critical Theory, he has practiced poetry for decades as an alternative text-medium to fiction and discursive prose. Literacy, the interplay of media, and the theory and architecture of prevailing cultural systems have, over recent decades, been his driving interests. Drawing their impetus from French theory and twentieth-century philosophy, the Frankfurt School, and psychoanalysis, his writings about literature largely concentrated on Euro-American modernism and its austere aftermath. Ongoing research created occasions for extended travel. His most recent work of cultural criticism is *The Great Dismissal: Memoir of the Cultural Demolition Derby, 2015-22* (Bloomsbury Academic, 2023). October, 2023 saw the premier of his play, "Soirée at Walter Benjamin's," in the Winterfest season of the New York Theater Festival. *Polaroids of Turbulence* is a debut volume of poetry.

Made in the USA
Columbia, SC
07 May 2024

34887735R00052